Christmas Roots

A coloring adventure for all

Jeanette Wummel

Coloring Tip:

When coloring with markers place a piece of paper between pages to prevent bleeding to your next design.

Acknowledgments

Christmas is such a fun time of the year. I have many cherish memories of Christmas
This book is dedicated to all those who can never get enough Christmas. Thank you for
being you and never change. I would like to give a big thank you to all the people who
have supported and encouraged me in making my dreams come true.

Follow me

Website/Blog:
www.TheRootsofDesign.com

Facebook:
www.facebook.com/TheRootsofDesign

Facebook Group:
www.facebook.com/group/ColoringRoots

Instagram:
www.instagram.com/therootsofdesign

Twitter:
https://twitter.com/Roots_Of_Design

Etsy:
www.RootsDesign.Etsy.com

Patreon:
www.patreon.com/RootsOfDesign

Copyright

This Book Belongs To:

_____

Bonus Pages

The following pages are some of the previous designs, but done in midnight style printed on black pages for your enjoyment.

Want More?

Check out my other books and more on
Amazon and Etsy, and
www.TheRootsOfDesign.com

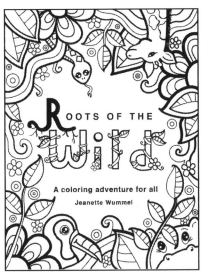

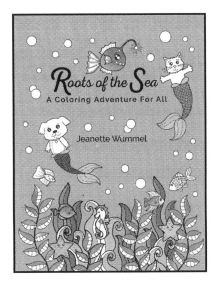

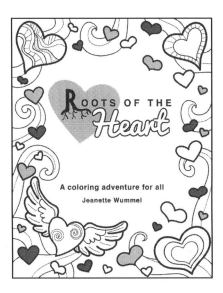

Made in the USA
Lexington, KY
10 August 2017